Lingo Dingo
and the
Turkish chef

Written by Mark Pallis

Illustrated by James Cottell

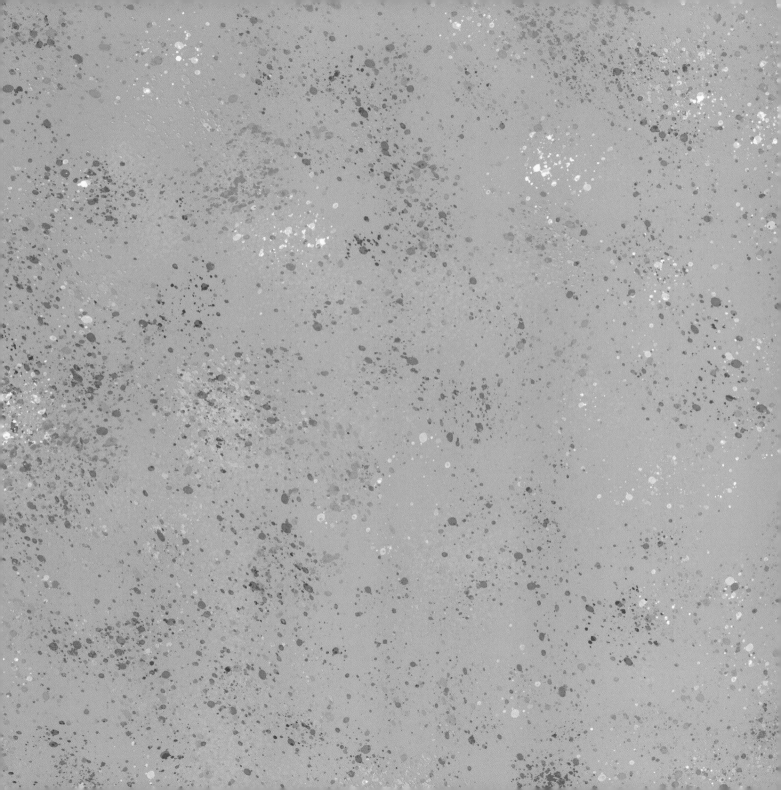

For my awesome sons - MP

For Leo and Juniper - JC

LINGO DINGO AND THE TURKISH CHEF

Story edited by Natascha Biebow, Blue Elephant Storyshaping
First Printing, 2023
ISBN: 978-1-915337-49-8
Neu Westend Press

Lingo Dingo
and the
Turkish chef

Written by Mark Pallis

Illustrated by James Cottell

NEU WESTEND
— PRESS —

This is Lingo. She's a Dingo and she loves helping.
Anyone. Anytime. Anyhow.

Lingo often helps her stylish neighbour Gunther, who lives by himself next door. She does a few jobs and has a nice chat. It makes Gunther feel good and it makes Lingo feel good too.

One day, Lingo arranged a special birthday party for Gunther. She even ordered a cake from a famous Turkish chef.

There was a knock at the door, "It must be the cake!" said Lingo.
But it was a monkey.

"Merhaba. Benim adım Şef Nono.
Benim bir sorunum var," he said.

Oh no. I can't speak Turkish yet, thought
Lingo. *Maybe 'merhaba' is like 'hello'.*

Merhaba = hello; **Benim adım** = my name is;
Benim bir sorunum var = I have a problem

"Merhaba," said Lingo. Chef Nono replied slowly,
"Üzgünüm ama doğum günü pastasını yapamam."

"I don't understand," said Lingo. "But let me guess. You want..."

Üzgünüm = I am sorry; **pastasını yapamam** = birthday cake;
doğum günü pastasını yapamam = I cannot make the birthday cake

Servis arabası mı = a trolley; Salatalık turşusu mu = a gherkin;
Balonlar mı = balloons; Hayır = no

"Fırınım bozuldu," explained Chef Nono.
"Fırınını kullanabilir miyim?"

Chef's oven must be broken thought Lingo. "I know!
Let's bake the cake together," she said.

Fırınım = my oven; bozuldu = is broken;
posso = can I; Fırınını kullanabilir miyim? = can I use your oven?

Chef tapped his wrist. "Saat kaç? Dokuz mu? On mu?" he asked.

Lingo showed Chef her watch.

"On bir mi? Hadi başlayalım! Çabuk!"
They only had one hour until the party.

Saat kaç? = what time is it?; Dokuz mu = nine o'clock; On mu = ten o'clock;
On bir mi = eleven o'clock; Hadi başlayalım = let's get started; Çabuk = quick

Chef Nono and Lingo whizzed around the kitchen:

İşte sana bir önlük.

Bir çırpıcı.

Bir kase.

İşte sana bir önlük = here's an apron; **Bir çırpıcı** = a whisk;
Bir kase = a mixing bowl

"Tereyağını, şekeri, yumurtaları ve unu ver lütfen," said Chef.

Lingo wasn't sure what those words meant, so she just grabbed fish, coffee and onions instead.

"Balık, kahve ve soğanlar. İğrenç!!" laughed Chef.

Chef plopped butter, sugar, eggs and flour into a bowl. "So that's what 'Tereyağını, şekeri, yumurtaları ve unu' means!" laughed Lingo.

"Karıştırıyorum, karıştırıyorsun, karıştırıyoruz," said Chef and together they began to mix the cake.

Karıştırıyorum = I mix; **karıştırıyorsun** = you mix; **karıştırıyoruz** = we mix

"Son olarak da kabartma tozu. İki kaşık," said Chef. Lingo guessed 'kabartma tozu' meant baking powder, but how much?

Before she could ask, Chef hurried away, saying, "Pardon, çişimi yapmam gerekiyor."

Lingo laughed, "I can guess what 'çişimi yapmam gerekiyor' means!"

Son olarak = finally; **kabartma tozu** = baking powder;
İki kaşık = two spoonfuls; **pardoni** = excuse me; **çişimi yapmam gerekiyor** = I need to do a wee wee

I wonder if this is too much? thought Lingo as she added ten spoonfulls of 'kabartma tozu' to the mix.

She carefully put everything into the oven and before long, a sweet cakey smell filled the kitchen.

kabartma tozu = baking powder

"Ne oldu? Bu kocaman!" said Chef.

Lingo realised she had added too much baking powder.
"Sorry," she said sheepishly.

Ne oldu = what happened; **Bu kocaman** = it is huge

They somehow got the cake out of the oven but ...

it was so big ...

... they couldn't hold it. "Disaster!" cried Lingo. "Bu bir felaket!" wailed Chef.

bu bir felaket = It's a disaster

"I know what will make you feel better," said Lingo, kindly. "Eat this 'Salatalık turşusu.'"

"İğrenç. Salatalık turşusundan nefret ederim." said Chef.

They were running out of time.

İğrenç = disgusting; **Salatalık turşusundan nefret ederim** = I hate gherkins

"I've got it! Gunther loves hats, so let's turn the cakey mess into a hat cake!" said Lingo.

First she shaped the cake, then she filled balloons with icing.

Next came the best part: POP! POP! POP!

It was a messy job but in the end, the cake looked fantastic.
"Kırmızı, turuncu, sari, yeşil, mavi. Muhteşem!" said Chef.

Kırmızı = red; **turuncu** = orange; **sari** = yellow;
yeşil = green; **mavi** = blue; **Muhteşem** = marvellous

There was a knock at the door.
"Kapı!" said Chef.
It was Gunther, and he was
wearing his special hat!

"Thank you. This makes me
feel so special," said Gunther.
"You are special," replied Lingo.

Kapı = the door

Gunther was thrilled with his cake.

Chef's deep voice sang "Doğum günün kutlu olsun...."

Doğum günün kutlu olsun = happy birthday to you

"Üfle !" said Chef.

Gunther blew out all the candles in one puff and everyone tucked in.

Üfle = blow

"Yiyorum, yiyorsun, o yiyor, o yiyor, onlar yiyorlar," laughed Chef.
"Biz yiyoruz," added Lingo proudly.

Yiyorum = I eat; **yiyorsun** = you eat; **o yiyor** = he eats;
o yiyor = she eats; **onlar yiyorlar** = they eat; **biz yiyoruz** = we eat

The friends watched the sun go down.

"Mutluyum,

mutlusun

Biz hepimiz mutluyuz!" cheered Chef.

Mutluyum = I am happy; **mutlusun** = you are happy;
Biz hepimiz mutluyuz = we are all happy

Baking a cake, helping a friend,
learning a new language... what a day!

But now it was time for bed. It was time to dream
about all the fun things that might happen tomorrow.

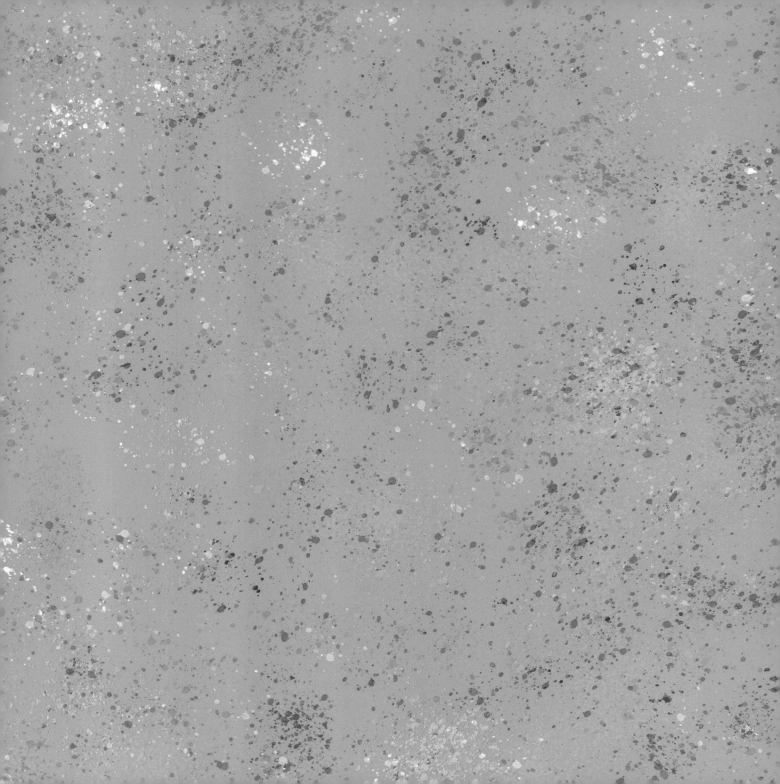

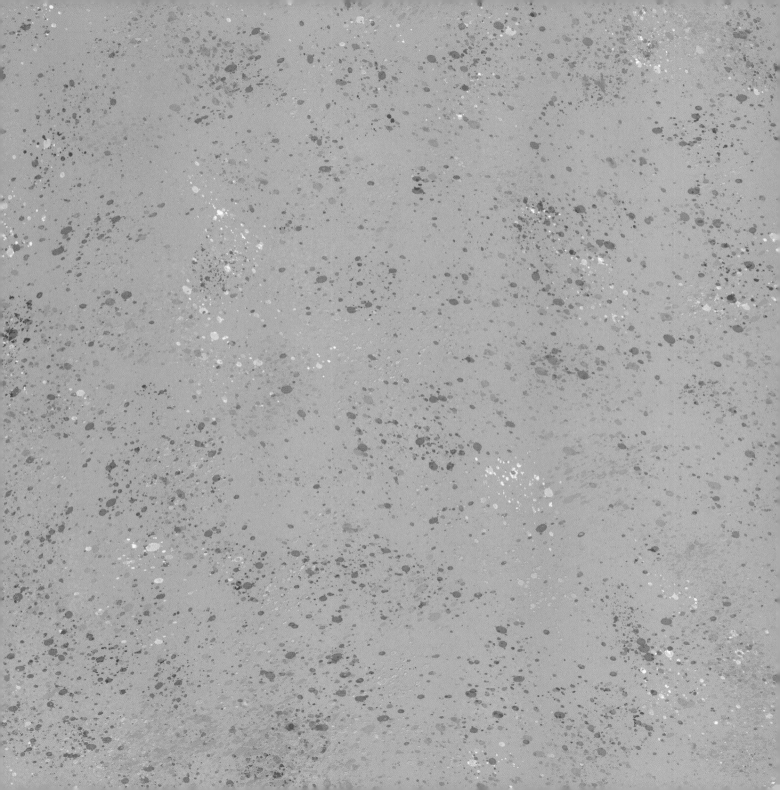

Learning to love languages

An additional language opens a child's mind, broadens their horizons and enriches their emotional life. Research has shown that the time between a child's birth and their sixth or seventh birthday is a "golden period" when they are most receptive to new languages. This is because they have an in-built ability to distinguish the sounds they hear and make sense of them. The Story-powered Language Learning Method taps into these natural abilities.

How the story-powered language learning method works

We create an emotionally engaging and funny story for children and adults to enjoy together, just like any other picture book. Studies show that social interaction, like enjoying a book together, is critical in language learning.

Through the story, we introduce a relatable character who speaks only in the new language. This helps build empathy and a positive attitude towards people who speak different languages. These are both important aspects in laying the foundations for lasting language acquisition in a child's life.

As the story progresses, the child naturally works with the characters to discover the meanings of a wide range of fun new words. Strategic use of humour ensures that this subconscious learning is rewarded with laughter; the child feels good and the first seeds of a lifelong love of languages are sown.

For more information and free learning resources visit www.markpallis.com

You can learn more words and phrases with these hilarious, heartwarming stories from NEU WESTEND — PRESS —

Also available in and many more languages!

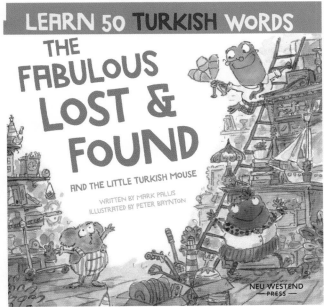

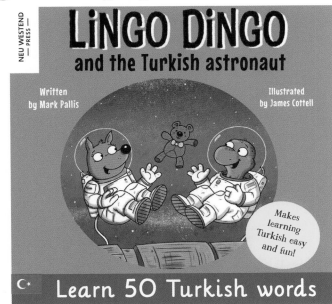

> "I want people to be so busy laughing, they don't realise they're learning!"
>
> Mark Pallis

Crab and Whale is the bestselling story of how a little Crab helps a big Whale. It's carefully designed to help even the most energetic children find a moment of calm and focus. It also includes a special mindful breathing exercise and affirmation for children.
Also available in Italian as 'Granchio e Balena'.
Featured as one of Mindful.org's
'Seven Mindful Children's books'

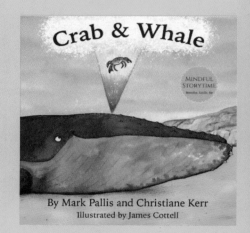

Do you call them hugs or cuddles?

In this funny, heartwarming story, you will laugh out loud as two loveable gibbons try to figure out if a hug is better than a cuddle and, in the process, learn how to get along.

A perfect story for anyone who loves a hug (or a cuddle!)

www.markpallis.com

Printed in Great Britain
by Amazon

In the Net!

Written by Jillian Powell
Photographs by Steve Lumb

Collins

I can pick it up.

I can kick it.

I can nod it.

I can rock it.

I can run.

I can run and tag.

I can get it.

Can I kick it in?

I can kick it in!

It is in the net!

I can get the cup.

I can pin it up.

In the net

Ideas for reading

Written by Clare Dowdall, PhD
Lecturer and Primary Literacy Consultant

Learning objectives: hear and say sounds in the order in which they occur; read simple words by sounding out and blending the phonemes all through the word from left to right; read some high frequency words; read a range of familiar and common words and simple sentences independently; show an understanding of how information can be found in non-fiction texts to answer questions about where, who, why and how; use phonic knowledge to write simple regular words and make phonetically plausible attempts at more complex words

Curriculum links: Physical Development: Move with control and coordination

Focus phonemes: i, c, a, n, p, ck, t, k, o, d, r, u, g, e, s

Fast words: I, the

Word count: 54

Getting started

- On a whiteboard, write the words *net, kick, can, run* and practise blending the sounds.

- Focus on the *k* and *ck* in *kick* and *c* in *can*. Remind children that they make the same sound, but are formed differently.

- Hand out the books and look at the front cover together. Read the title, practising to blend the sounds.

- Ask children to suggest what the title means, what the book might be about and whether they think it is fiction or non-fiction.

Reading and responding

- Ask children to read the blurb, focusing on blending individual words.

- Ask children to read the book through to p13 using their blending skills to decode new words.

- Support children as they read. Remind children to blend through new words, e.g. *n-o-d nod* and to reread for fluency.

- Ask fast-finishers to reread the book fluently, using the punctuation.